THE FATHER SERIES

www.justinandabi.com/thefatherseries/redeem

Check out our podcast, The Connected Life!

The Connected Life is a thought-provoking conversation about all the beautiful and messy ups and downs of life. Join Life Consultants Justin & Abi Stumvoll as they share vulnerable stories and practical wisdom that will lead you on a journey of connecting with yourself, others, and the world right in front of you. Their authentic, no-BS style will make you laugh, challenge you to dig deep, face your fears, and inspire you to love yourself and others more.

You can listen to The Connected Life Podcast on any of the following:

iTunes | Stitcher | Podcast Bean | Spotify

For more information about our other courses check out www.justinandabi.com

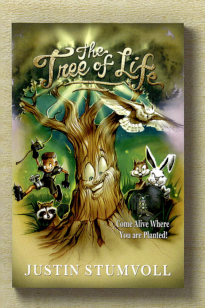

The Tree of Life is an allegory that chronicles the journey each of us must embark upon to find healing from the bumps and bruises incurred through life. The invitation resounding from *The Tree of Life* is for adults to return to the joys of imaginative innocence and it's a promise to children that everything they need to fulfill their dreams is within them. The message for everyone is that we must learn how to come alive wherever we find ourselves planted.

To get your copy go to: www.justinandabi.com/shop

Look with wonder at the depth of the Father's marvelous love that he has lavished on us! He has called us and made us his very own beloved children.

—JOHN 3:1

THE FATHER SERIES

A TWELVE-PART WORKBOOK

JUSTIN AND ABI STUMVOLL

WITH BLAIR REYNOLDS

© 2019 by Justin and Abi Stumvoll

All Scripture quotations, unless otherwise notated, are from The Passion Translation®. Copyright © 2017, 2018 by Passion & Fire Ministries, Inc. Used by permission. All rights reserved. ThePassionTranslation.com.

Emphasis to Scripture has been added by the author.

ISBN: 978-1-949709-50-6

INTRODUCTION **9**

EPISODE ONE
THE IMPORTANCE OF DIALOGUING ABOUT FATHERS **19**

EPISODE TWO
THE ATTRIBUTES OF A HEALTHY FATHER **29**

EPISODE THREE
THE EFFECTS OF FATHERS ON THEIR DAUGHTERS **39**

EPISODE FOUR
THE EFFECTS OF FATHERS ON THEIR SONS **49**

EPISODE FIVE
FINDING WHOLENESS AFTER BEING HURT: SPECIAL GUEST PAUL YOUNG **57**

EPISODE SIX
CONFRONTING OUR FATHERS: HOPE FOR HEALING AND CONNECTION **67**

EPISODE SEVEN
LAYING TO REST OUR FATHER WOUNDS **77**

EPISODE EIGHT
STORIES OF GOOD FATHERS **87**

EPISODE NINE
RETURNING TO CHILDLIKENESS **97**

EPISODE TEN
FATHER GOD **99**

EPISODE ELEVEN
COMPASSION FOR FATHERS: GUEST DANNY MARTINEZ **109**

EPISODE TWELVE
MOVING FORWARD: STEPS TO FORGIVENESS **127**

CONCLUSION **141**

FOREWORD

A decade ago, I was in the car reading *The Shack* out loud to my wife. There is a point in the book when Papa (a big black woman representing Father God) turns into an older man. When this transition happened, I burst into tears. Confused, Abi asked me what was going on. After several moments of pulling myself back together I was able to say, "As soon as Papa turned into a man I felt connection with him disappear. Now he feels cold, disinterested, and disengaged towards Mack (the main character)." That is the moment I realized that I had pain I wasn't aware of from relationships with men in my life.

I wanted to deal with the pain so that I could heal. I asked several of my mentors about what I should do to move forward. The only resource they knew of was a book I had already read. Without a roadmap, I jumped into a decade-long journey of facing my pain and fears so that love could make me whole again.

What I didn't know when I first started was that I was jumping into a rabbit hole. I soon began to see that the undercurrent of pain that I had never acknowledged was driving every area of my life. It affected my worth, confidence, ability to take risks, and how I viewed my future. It affected how I did and viewed business, finances, friendship, marriage, God, and so much more. I realized that in order to receive love and be fulfilled, I needed to experience and understand good fathering.

In case you've wondered, you can't just find a good father and force him to adopt you. And honestly, if you have pain or rejection from fathers, you often show up with a sign on your forehead inviting more rejection from the men around you. This becomes infuriating as it feels like you're trapped in a never-ending loop that can't get resolved, needing something that you don't know how to get.

The healing journey wasn't an easy overnight process for me. In order to get out, I had to take ownership for the lies and cycles I had been in. I had to vulnerably share and invite people into my pain and weakness. I had to have straightforward conversations with my family and men that had affected me. I had to set boundaries, forgive, and learn about my value. I had to soften my heart and allow God to reveal to me what His nature as a good and unconditionally loving father is actually like.

This process has brought me hope, joy, and fulfillment in a way I never dreamed was possible. It doesn't mean I'm a guru and I know everything there is to know now. However, I will say that this journey has changed everything about how my life looks and feels.

There is a concept that leadership starts with making your ceiling someone else's floor. Because of the amazing benefits of going through all of this, I became passionate about helping others find the same freedom by making my ceiling their floor. This same passion is shared by the love of my life, Abi, and Blair Reynolds. It's our hope that in teaming up we could gather our collective knowledge and share the best of what we had in order to help others walk out that same journey in a fraction of the time it took us.

Paul Young says that it took him 50 years to wipe the face of his father off of the face of God. If this is any sort of signpost, I am sure that I will continue to discover the immensity of Father God's goodness for the rest of my life. In all that I've learned and have to share, I believe I've only taken the initial steps of this life-long journey. Because of this, I have learned to surrender to an indescribable grace that leads me daily, knowing I can't fix myself, but I can invite love to have its way in me.

This e-course is an invitation for you to do the same.

INTRODUCTION TO

THE FATHER SERIES

As you take these initial steps, your life is about to become better than it's ever been. In order to get there, emotions, thoughts, and memories may spring up. You might feel raw and a bit messy in the process. But that's normal. On the other side of it there is the healing and restoration you've been wanting and needing. Blair, Abi, and I love digging into heart issues, but we also think that life is meant to be fun and playful. Because of this, there are tons of laughs and fun sprinkled into all the emotional stuff.

This is not an instruction manual outlining how to fix everything in your life that went wrong because of your father. Heck, it's not even an instruction manual on how to repair your relationship with your dad (although we do give some great tips). It's more like a guided invitation to help you to look honestly at your life as you consider what's been hiding under the rug that has been tripping you up. Oh yeah, it's also a tool belt, filled with a bunch of tools to help you get started on the process of healing and growth.

YOU CAN EXPECT TO WALK AWAY FROM THIS SERIES WITH:

- A greater capacity to give and receive love
- More compassion toward yourself and others
- Revelation about forgiveness and the necessary tools to forgive
- More clarity about your purpose
- A deeper level of confidence
- More Freedom

Everyone has their own unique circumstances when it comes to a father. There are those who grew up in two-parent homes with awesome, mediocre, or abusive dads. Perhaps you were given up for adoption or placed in the foster care system. You may have had a single mom, lesbian mothers, or been fathered through a sperm donor. Well, you get the point. There is a myriad of circumstances regarding fathers and children, and we won't be able to cover every single instance.

What we will address are the universal wounds and pain we have regarding our fathers, or lack thereof. That father may be your dad, mom's boyfriend(s), or a male authority that you perceived as a father figure in your life. Regardless, your job is to apply the information in this series to your circumstance. You get to decide how it relates to you as well as how it can help you find healing and freedom.

**When we ask questions about your father, don't feel limited to only answering about an official "father" in your life. Write about any of the men in your life who affected you in the areas we are discussing.

This series is also for the people who grew up with a good dad. In fact, if you've had a great dad, this series is perfect for you. It means you already have a solid foundation, and this book will help your relationship delve to greater depths of communication and connection!

This is NOT A RULE BOOK, but a helpful guide. People often take information that is meant to help them and turn the tips into rigid rules on "How to live." We give examples of how to process pain or how to connect to love that are meant to inspire and provoke you. This series is not a comprehensive guide on the exact way every person must process in order to grow. If the concepts and conversations in this series become universal laws where you stop considering other perspectives, then they will become an anchor around your neck. Let it be what it is, a helpful guide.

Some of you may feel ashamed of your circumstances. This shame may be the reason you haven't taken time to look at your history concerning a father. We are all super messy. In fact, that's the beauty of our humanity. No one, and no one's circumstances are perfect. We are all in the same boat. Every person needs love and affirmation, and we all have experienced heartache and loss. Know that you are not alone, you are not behind, and you are not the only person with brokenness. You are in the exact place you need to be right now. This is the right moment in your life to experience more love than ever before.

What community broke can be healed through community. Where one father failed you, others will be part of the redemption process. The point is that you are not alone! Freedom does not come through hiding out and pretending it is entirely up to us to heal ourselves. We invite you to let go of your shame. If you embark on this journey openly and invite others into the places you've been avoiding, you will experience acceleration into wholeness.

If while you are going through this workbook, you realize that you need someone to walk with you and help you through this process, we have a team of consultants that we recommend. They have spent years working through their father pain and can help you as you go. Information for them, as well as other resources for healing can be found in the "Conclusion" at the back of the book.

Last but not least, get excited. Everyone in this series has gone on this journey. Because of it, we are all living happier, healthier lives. That is a great indication of where you are headed as well!

Cheering you on,

Blair Reynolds, Justin and Abi Stumvoll

PRACTICAL NOTE TO REMEMBER WHILE ANSWERING QUESTIONS THROUGHOUT THIS SERIES:

Take as much time as you need. Sometimes it takes a minute for memories to come back. Asking someone who knew your family for more information about your history can be helpful. We have found that many of our clients have forgotten what childhood was like. Dialoguing with others helped them remember.

If writing overwhelms you, listen to the episodes and then dialogue about the questions with your friends. If you feel overwhelmed by the questions, just do one at a time, or skip a question and come back later. Don't get stuck. If you need to listen to the next episode and keep moving on, then do that.

These questions are meant to help you absorb and put into application what you are learning. They are meant to benefit you, not become the homework you always avoided in high school. Everyone's personality is different. Do whatever you need to do to enjoy this series.

(From Abi who is dyslexic and knows that everyone has a different learning style.)

LEADING A SMALL GROUP

So you've decided to lead a small group!!! YAY!!!! We love that so much and believe this series will produce the best results in a small group setting. The healing process is expedited when we do it with community!

God made each of us unique, and we know that each person has a different leadership style. While we don't want to cramp that style, we do want to set you up for success whether you have led a group in the past or not. Below are some suggestions we think could help you lead a small group. Feel free to use what works for you and throw out whatever doesn't. This is meant to be helpful, not create rules that burden you.

We recommend gathering a group of around five people. That way each group member will have time to share the nitty-gritty stuff without feeling rushed. (Five is not a magic number so plus or minus is fine). If this series is going to be used in a larger, ongoing group, consider splitting into the same groups each meeting for the discussions.

We suggest having weekly meetings and that each person listens to one audio episode per week and fills in the corresponding questions outside of the group time. We've found that when people listen to the audio privately, they are able to connect to their thoughts and emotions more deeply. They are less distracted and self-conscious in their own spaces.

Doing the workbook prior to the group meeting is tremendously beneficial as it helps participants feel prepared, have language for their emotions, and feel connected to what is being discussed. Note: If they forget or don't have time to fill in the questions, they can still be a part of the discussion.

SET YOUR GROUP UP FOR SUCCESS:

1. As a leader, it is your job to set the tone. The people in your group will be as vulnerable as you are. Let them know they're in a safe place where they can be vulnerable. Lead by example. Safety and vulnerability are the foundation for building a group of people who are willing to be open and honest.

2. The fastest way to shatter trust is to regurgitate sacred information outside of a sacred space. This is gossip, and gossip is one of the most destructive forces to intimacy and honesty. Clarify to the group that the space is a confidential and holy ground where gossip in any form is unacceptable. Doing so will be terms for being asked to leave the group.

3. Let your group know that the goal is for everyone to have time to share and be heard. This is a game changer as most groups have a "talker". There may be times when someone is sharing and you need to ask, *"Can you wrap this thought/story up in the next minute or so?"* This ensures that everyone gets a chance. (If you set ground rules before it happens, then they won't take it as personally.) We have used this statement many times in meetings. While it can feel awkward at first, it becomes normal and everyone appreciates it. Fear of interrupting the talker in order to avoid hurt feelings can leave the others feeling forgotten. Remember that your job as the leader is to care for each person's heart.

4. Tell the group that it is NOT their job to fix everyone's pain. We can't. This series is designed to stir up the wounding that has been driving our lives. If someone shares and people try to fix the problem, it can feel invalidating. Many respond to this by shutting down. This series has many tools, but they are given sporadically in the episodes. Trying to fix something may shortcut another person's process. We recommend communicating that group members are meant to listen with compassion and love. It will most likely be necessary to remind the group to not try to fix each other as more is shared along the way. Let them know that if anyone starts to feel shut down, there is permission to stop and communicate with the group. Model for them a way to share that they just need to be heard and do not need an answer.

5. If someone shares something raw or vulnerable, be sure to have a kind, compassionate, and gentle response. If someone is sobbing, give them a moment, maybe even a hug if needed. Before moving on, let them know that you are really proud of their vulnerability.

6. If something is happening that you don't know how to handle or that you don't understand, communicate: *"I don't know how to respond to this, simply because this is new to me. I want you to know that we all love you and care about you. Is there anything you need?"* Most often people's responses are along these lines: "I need to be held. I need to be told that I am going to be okay. I need to be told that I am lovable. I need you to pray for me."

7. Sometimes, they may answer that they don't know what they need. In this case you can ask questions. *"Do you need a hug, to hear that you are going to be okay, to hear that you are lovable, or to have us pray for you?"*

8. There may be a need that you cannot meet: "I need for my pain to be gone, or I need to punch my dad." You can communicate that while you can't meet that need, there are a few that you can. (Punching pillows works well.) Give them options that you can do. Holy Spirit is fantastic at coming up with creative solutions and questions in the moment. Give Him space to speak and do not be afraid of silence from time to time. If you don't know how or what to pray, here is an example of a simple prayer: *"Papa God, thank You for what You're doing. We invite You to continue to love on and heal (name of person). We welcome Your healing, grace, and truth to this part of their journey. Amen."*

9. Remember that it is not your group's job to fix everyone's pain, and it certainly is not yours either. You have said yes to lead and to create space for people to continue into whole-hearted living. Have fun, do not take yourself too seriously, and remember that each group member's process will look different. You are not responsible for their lives or their journeys. You get to listen, love, pray, and share the heart of the Father. You have permission to not know all the answers and to ask for help from the people around you. You can do this!

YOUR FIRST SMALL GROUP MEETING:

Here is a general outline to get you started. Feel free to be creative and personalize it for you and your group:

- Have an opportunity to casually socialize before the meeting begins (snacks or icebreaker activities are great meeting starters)
- Have each person share about themselves for approximately 3 minutes
- Introduce guidelines and core values for this group (suggestions listed above in the section, "Things to Remember")
- Have each person share their personal history with their father(s) to get an idea of their background and experiences (Limit sharing to 5 minutes)
- Explain which audio they need to listen to before the next meeting, and what questions/activations will be discussed

WEEKLY MEETINGS:

1. *What was one "Aha" moment that you had listening to this episode?* (Have each person answer.)

2. *Did you experience any triggers?* (See info about triggers on page 16.)

3. Pick two questions or activations (or one of both) from the workbook to ask the whole group. You can tell the group you're asking these questions in advance (the week before) or ask them spontaneously in the meetings. Varying the types of questions asked each week will help it feel balanced. (A few heavy questions and a few lighter questions.)

TRIGGERS:

Triggers are moments where you have a strong or disproportionate emotional response to what you are hearing or experiencing. You may feel angry, irritated, sad, or like you want to quit listening and think about something else. Do not freak out if you have a strong response. There is simply an invitation to come into a deeper place of healing. Triggers let you know that the material is pushing against emotions or a belief system that may have been suppressed and needs attention.

Sometimes, you notice triggers right away. If you start feeling a strong emotion that seems out of proportion to the information you are hearing, write down the content of the episode and what you were thinking about in response. You want to have as many clues as possible as to what caused your reaction.

Sometimes triggers show up later as a huge emotional response to something that is relatively small. For instance, maybe later that day, the next day, or a week later you find yourself exploding at a friend who forgot to ask how your day was going. You cannot fathom why you're a level-8-angry about a level-1-infraction until you realize the root. You're really sad and angry that your dad never asked you about your day. Your high emotions are not really about what happened with your friend but about memories and pain that came up while listening to an episode or participating in your group.

EPISODE ONE

THE IMPORTANCE OF DIALOGUING ABOUT FATHERS

I lie awake each night thinking of you and reflecting on how you help me like a father.

-PSALM 63:6

SUMMARY

In this introduction to *The Father Series*, Justin, Abi, and Blair dive into why processing pain from our fathers is critical for all of our lives. They explore the attributes of a good father and the detrimental repercussions for a child who experiences life without these qualities.

With a firm sense of hope, they discuss how freedom from our wounds is possible, but only through the necessary process of unveiling and unlocking the places of pain inside of ourselves that have long laid buried and dormant.

QUESTIONS FROM THE EPISODE

1. What did my dad's actions, reactions, and words teach me to believe about myself?

2. How would my perception of myself be different if I had felt my identity affirmed consistently by my dad? If my dad consistently affirmed me, what did that teach me about myself?

3. What pain that stems from my dad have I been avoiding?

4. What excuses have I used to avoid "being vulnerably honest" about the negative experiences with him? (Example: *He was doing the best he knew how. He could have been much worse. The past is the past, and I should leave it there. There's no point in looking into those things. Nothing will change, etc.*)

5. Where in my life have I projected my own experience with my father onto God, authority figures, or other people?

6. Were there areas in my life where I felt shut down in my childhood? Which of those areas do I still feel shut down in today? (Example: *My father never listened to me, and I still believe that no one will ever listen to me.*)

7. How did the way I was disciplined impact the way I view the world and God? (Example: *When I made mistakes as a kid, I was never given patience and understanding. Now when I make mistakes, I believe that I am a burden and an irritation to people.*)

_____
_____
_____
_____
_____
_____
_____

8. What are the costs today for me not processing the damage from my father? (Example: *I always feel like powerful people won't like me. I'm not teachable. I'm always getting into arguments with authority figures, etc.*)

_____
_____
_____
_____
_____
_____
_____

> "WHENEVER YOU HAVE EMOTIONS DISPROPORTIONATE TO THE PRESENT, IT MEANS THEY ARE ROOTED IN THE PAST."

CONNECTING TO GOD AS FATHER

How do you view Father God? In your perception, what is His personality like?

_____
_____
_____
_____
_____
_____
_____
_____
_____
_____
_____
_____
_____
_____

ACTIVATIONS

ACTIVATION ONE:

Inside each of us is a voice disconnected from our lists of rules and shoulds. It consists of the feelings and opinions we hide when we believe we will get rejected or hurt by sharing. This voice includes the thoughts and feelings we don't want to admit we feel and those we have judged illogical.

For the sake of this activation, we will call this voice your heart. It has been proven that when you place your hand over your heart you share more honestly. We have found that when people ask or invite their heart to speak, it allows them to access their subconscious beliefs and feelings more easily.

In this activation, let your heart know you are ready to hear about its pain. Give yourself permission to go on a journey of uncovering places that have been shut down and disconnected due to unprocessed pain from your father.

Set an alarm on your phone for once a day. Tell your heart, *"Heart, I am listening to you. Your pain matters to me, and your experience matters to me. Heart, I give you permission to communicate the places you have disappointment and hurt that you need to face. Heart, I give you permission to receive love in those places of pain and sadness."*

There are several different ways you may hear from your heart. Sometimes you may not sense anything and then randomly that day or week, something will really trigger you. You may have high emotions or raging thoughts about a situation that doesn't warrant that degree of response. As you process the event, you may realize that your frustration is actually about something from your childhood, not from the current situation. An example of a trigger would be finding out that your friend is moving and being completely devastated by it. You realize that you love your friend but are also aware that this much grief is illogical. As you deal with more, you realize that the hurt is intense because it pushes on the pain that remains from your dad abandoning you.

Here are a few other ways that you may hear from your heart: You could have a dream about something that brings up an ache that won't quit. A wave of emotions may wash over you randomly. You may also have past thoughts, memories, and emotions come to your mind either right away or later on after you give your heart permission to have a voice.

When feelings and thoughts begin to come up, choose to sit in them. The goal is to become present and aware. Write down what comes up. So often we disengage from the emotions and memories that come up when we talk about pain. Culturally, we are often taught to shove the discomfort and sadness away. We can temporarily avoid feeling our sadness by distracting ourselves or engaging in unhealthy coping mechanisms.

ACTIVATION TWO:

Spend 15 minutes daily for the next week with just you and your internal world. Try to be fully present with yourself. Turn off your cell phone or put it on airplane mode. Leave the TV off, and go somewhere with minimal distractions. If sadness arises, allow yourself to feel and connect to it. Invite Unconditional Love to come and bring you compassion and comfort.

NOTES

EPISODE TWO

THE ATTRIBUTES OF A HEALTHY FATHER

From a long distance away, his father saw him coming, dressed as a beggar, and great compassion swelled up in his heart for his son who was returning home. So the father raced out to meet him. He swept him up in his arms, hugged him dearly, and kissed him over and over with tender love.

Then the son said, "Father, I was wrong. I have sinned against you. I could never deserve to be called your son. Just let me be—"

The father interrupted and said, "Son, you're home now!"

Turning to his servants, the father said, "Quick, bring me the best robe, my very own robe, and I will place it on his shoulders. Bring the ring, the seal of sonship, and I will put it on his finger. And bring out the best shoes you can find for my son. Let's prepare a great feast and celebrate. For this beloved son of mine was once dead, but now he's alive again. Once he was lost, but now he is found!" And everyone celebrated with overflowing joy.

—LUKE 15:20-24

SUMMARY

Most of us do not have a great model for what it looks like to be fathered. Without a healthy blueprint, we can unknowingly recreate the cycle that caused us so much pain in the first place.

In this episode, Justin and Blair map out the qualities of masculine parenting and tackle why these aspects are so meaningful and deeply impacting to our lives. They discuss how we need to redefine fathering in order to get real and authentic healing.

QUESTIONS FROM THE EPISODE

1. What are the attributes of fathering that I missed in my life?

_____
_____
_____
_____
_____
_____
_____
_____
_____

2. What are three things my father did that were positive? What are three things I wish he had done differently?

_____
_____
_____
_____
_____
_____
_____
_____
_____

> "A FATHER IMPARTS IDENTITY,
> AND HE CAN ONLY IMPART IDENTITY WHEN HE IS
> CONFIDENT IN HIS OWN."

3. When asked each of the following questions, what is the first thought that comes to mind?

- What are the responsibilities of a father?
- How does a father feel about his children?
- How involved does a father want to be?

_____

4. From my answers in question 3, where did I form this stereotype? Do my conclusions lead to perceptions of men that keep me from connecting to safe father figures? If so, what are these perceptions?

_____

5. Did my father model gentleness and compassion to me? If not, what are the ways I have withheld those things from myself?

6. Does affection from a man feel safe to me? Why or why not?

7. When we grow up with a father who feels compassionate and powerful, then there is safety to make mistakes and grow. Are there places in my life where I've avoided taking risks because of fear of failure or of not having anyone to fall back on? If so, how would my life be different if I was unafraid of failure and confident that someone else is bigger than me and invested in my growth?

8. We often "parent" or treat ourselves the way we were parented. What was my dad's style of parenting? Are there connections between how my father parented me and how I treat myself? (Example: *My dad never paid attention to my wants or needs and so I never pay attention to my wants and needs.*)

_____
_____
_____
_____
_____
_____
_____

9. Did I feel believed in by my dad? Why or why not? Depending on my answer, how has that impacted the way I view my value and my capabilities?

_____
_____
_____
_____
_____
_____
_____

10. Regardless of how my dad believed in me, I get to choose to believe in me. What are some positive, true statements about my value and capabilities?

_____
_____
_____
_____
_____
_____
_____

CONNECTING TO GOD AS FATHER

1. How close do you feel to Father God?

2. Why do you believe there is intimacy, indifference, or disconnection in your relationship with Him?

ACTIVATIONS

ACTIVATION ONE:

When we imagine a scenario, our emotions do not perceive the difference between reality and fiction. This is why we can have bad emotions after visualizing bad things happening in our future, just like we can have positive emotions after visualizing good things happening.

Our painful past experiences can perpetuate torment when we repeatedly visualize them over the years. A powerful way to bring healing and redemption to our past is to imagine what we needed back then happening to us.

In this activation, visualize a time in your life when you wished your father could've been more engaged, gentle, or connected to you. Imagine a father figure or a movie character that exemplifies a safe, loving father. After choosing an ideal image, imagine him coming into that memory and giving you the love and the encouragement you needed in that moment. When you change your visualization of the memory, you can begin to experience different thoughts and emotions. This can help you begin to believe new truths.

ACTIVATION TWO:

If you were to have children just like you, what would you want them to know about themselves and how valuable they are? Write at least ten things you would say to them. Now read them over yourself as affirmations of the kind of love you are worthy of experiencing.

1. _____
2. _____
3. _____
4. _____
5. _____
6. _____
7. _____
8. _____
9. _____
10. _____

NOTES

THE FATHER SERIES / EPISODE THREE

*The next two episodes are targeted toward specific genders. However, listening to both is beneficial. You will hear things that help you understand those around you, and much of the information is applicable regardless of gender. Most of the questions and activations are gender neutral as well.

EPISODE THREE

THE EFFECTS OF FATHERS ON THEIR DAUGHTERS

Arise, my dearest. Hurry, my darling.
Come away with me!
I have come as you have asked
to draw you to my heart and lead you out.
For now is the time, my beautiful one.
The season has changed,
the bondage of your barren winter has ended,
and the season of hiding is over and gone.
—SONG OF SONGS 2:10-12

SUMMARY

In this episode Abi, Justin, and Blair tackle the topic of women with father wounds, how those wounds manifest, and what negative parental behavior created the wounds in the first place.

Through this open and honest dialogue, clarity and hope are provided for women to find healing. They also open the door for men to step in and be a part of this sensitive conversation.

QUESTIONS FROM THE EPISODE

1. When we have wounds, we often make generalizations and accusations to protect ourselves. What are three ways I have made conscious or unconscious judgments about men?

   _____
   _____
   _____
   _____
   _____

2. How does the hurt from my father manifest in relationships with men around me? (Example: *My dad never listened to me, so I find myself choosing to connect with men who are self-absorbed and never listen to me.*)

   _____
   _____
   _____
   _____
   _____

3. What kind of men do I have intense "chemistry" with or find myself naturally "pulled" towards? Is there a common dysfunction among them? What about their dysfunction draws me in, and how does this dysfunction relate to my dad?

   _____
   _____
   _____
   _____
   _____

4. Who are good/safe men in my world that I could have connection with? What are the ways my own lens could prevent me from seeing and identifying healthy men?

5. How did my mom interact with my father/father figure? How did my mom communicate about my father? How did this affect the way I have perceived him? How did this affect how I perceive men in general?

6. Did I grow up believing that one parent was a victim to the other parent? If so, how were they a victim in my perspective? How was the parent I see as a victim choosing to act powerless?

7. We develop coping skills by trying to protect ourselves from experiencing discomfort with our parents. What are three ways I learned to protect myself? Where are those coping skills showing up in my life now? (Example: *I learned to really dislike people who hurt me. I refuse to forgive them so I don't have to feel close to them or be hurt by them anymore. I learned to cut people out of my life and now that shows up by me ending relationships.*)

_____
_____
_____
_____
_____
_____

8. Blair discusses how logically naming and identifying healthy father-figure behavior can help us. List ten positive attributes of a father figure. Which men in my life have some of those positive qualities? In making this list, are there more good men surrounding me than I originally thought?

_____
_____
_____
_____
_____
_____
_____
_____
_____
_____
_____
_____
_____
_____
_____

9. **For Women:**

Often we have high needs and expectations from the men in our lives based on heartache from our fathers. We can sometimes believe that if the man/men in our lives meet our needs perfectly, then we will no longer have pain from our fathers. Can I see any areas in my relationships with men where my needs or expectations have been too high?

Bonus - If you're married or in a relationship:

Are there ways that I am unconsciously reacting to my parent during difficult conversations with my significant other? If so, which parent? What issue from my childhood is showing up in these moments? (Example: *When my spouse gets intense I immediately shut down because it reminds me of my mother who had out-of-control anger. Or, when my spouse is hurt I feel angry and defensive. I feel blamed because my father always misunderstood me and blamed me for things that weren't my fault. Or, when my partner and I are in conflict I get mean and reject them first because my father left, and I don't want to be abandoned again.*)

CONNECTING TO GOD AS FATHER

Justin talks about experiencing the feminine nature of God. Have there been traits that I've disconnected from God due to believing His characteristics are only masculine? (Example: *I haven't seen God as comforting, nurturing, or tender.*) Invite God to reveal the feminine traits of His nature to you.

ACTIVATIONS

ACTIVATION ONE:

Watch a movie that showcases strong and loving father figures. Engage your heart to experience men who are strong and safe. As you watch the movie, imagine yourself receiving the love and care the fathers are giving away.

Here is a list of shows that people have said helped them connect to something about a father's heart. We are not endorsing them and have not seen all of them, so your own discretion is required. We recommend you intentionally watch a movie about a good father from this list or one of your choosing every week of the course to help push buttons and bring healing.

- Movies: *Instant Family, Finding Nemo, The Martian Child, About Time, Life is Beautiful, Despicable Me 2, Meet the Robinson's, Mrs. Doubtfire, I Am Sam, Frequency, The Shack, John Q, The Pursuit of Happyness, Taken, The Blindside, Hook, Lion King, The Guardian, Courageous, We Bought a Zoo, Family Man, Father of the Bride 1 & 2, Juno, Swiss Family Robinson, To Kill A Mockingbird*

- Movies with great father figures: *Batman Begins* (both Bruce Wayne and Alfred), *Three Men and a Baby, Three Men and a Little Lady, Good Will Hunting*

- TV show: *This Is Us*

ACTIVATION TWO:

Do I need to apologize and ask for forgiveness from any men in my life for having unrealistic expectations due to wounding from my father? Are there men who consistently disappoint me no matter what they do? If so, write a letter, make a phone call, or go see them and apologize.

ACTIVATION THREE (FOR COUPLES ONLY):

Abi talks about making sure you are receiving love from the people trying to love you. Have your spouse/significant other say ten declarations of love and value over you. Repeat the declarations, and agree with the spirit of love over yourself. Allow yourself to connect to and receive those positive truths.

NOTES

EPISODE FOUR

THE EFFECTS OF FATHERS ON THEIR SONS

And you did not receive the "spirit of religious duty," leading you back into the fear of never being good enough. But you have received the "Spirit of full acceptance," enfolding you into the family of God. And you will never feel orphaned, for as he rises up within us, our spirits join him in saying the words of tender affection, "Beloved Father!" For the Holy Spirit makes God's fatherhood real to us as he whispers into our innermost being, "You are God's beloved child!"

—ROMANS 8:15-16

SUMMARY

The relationship between a son and his father can be a source of life or the battleground for a life-long war. The actions and words of our fathers have the power to propel us to the peak of success, and in the same breath, be the very downfall of our dreams.

In this episode, Blair and Justin discuss the impact Tiger Woods' father had on him and how Tiger's unprocessed pain and unforgiveness eventually led to his breakdown and downfall. Though Tiger's life seems unique, the lessons from his life are universal.

QUESTIONS FROM THE EPISODE

1. What do I believe is a healthy father's role in a young man or woman's life?

2. What areas did I feel not "good enough" for my father? Do I believe this was a real expectation or a perceived one, and why?

3. Have you ever felt abandoned or neglected by your father? How and when? What was your reaction at the time? When you think about those experiences now, what happens internally?

4. Are there areas where I am pursuing ambition or trying to be perfect in order to win my father's approval? If so, what are they?

5. What are healthy ways to be driven and pursue success in life? (Example: *For the joy of creating, for the joy of expressing myself.*) Have you experienced these "healthy ambitions" before? When and where did you experience them?

6. What does ideal connection look like in my relationship with my father (or father figure)? How would I relate to him? How would we communicate with one another?

CONNECTING TO GOD AS FATHER

1. What are the emotions that you think Father God feels toward you? (Example: *He tolerates me. He loves me but is too busy for me.*)

   _____
   _____
   _____
   _____
   _____
   _____
   _____

2. What are the emotions you would want God to feel towards you? (Example: *He is proud of me and loves me unconditionally. He loves showing me off to His friends. He loves to hear what I think about things. He loves partnering with me, He loves how I pray, etc.*)

   _____
   _____
   _____
   _____
   _____
   _____
   _____

3. What are the emotions you feel toward Father God? What thoughts do you think about Him?

   _____
   _____
   _____
   _____
   _____
   _____
   _____

ACTIVATIONS

ACTIVATION ONE:

Write a letter (that you don't intend to deliver) to your father about the places where you needed a dad but he never showed up. Be brutally honest, as this is purely to help you process your thoughts and emotions. If, after expressing everything that needs to be purged, you find yourself wanting to send it, wait until you listen to Episode 6. Then rewrite the letter in a way that feels honest, yet honoring in how you express your truth.

ACTIVATION TWO:

Visualize a life where loving and powerful men who believe in you surround you. How would you think, feel, or act differently than you do now? How can you start living that life now?

Example: *If there were compassionate and powerful men around me, I would be safe to fail. If I felt safe to fail, I would take more risks and know that I would be okay. I am now going to go act like I would if that visualization were true. I'm going to imagine that feeling of safety and then go take a risk.*

Example: *If I felt like men were for me not against me, I would look them in the eyes with confidence when I spoke to them. This week, I am going to look men in the eyes and imagine that they are for me.*

> "CHILDHOOD IS LIKE AN ALPHABET.
> THAT ALPHABET WILL FORM WORDS.
> THOSE WORDS WILL FORM SENTENCES.
> THOSE SENTENCES WILL FORM
> THE STORY OF OUR LIVES."

NOTES

EPISODE FIVE

FINDING WHOLENESS AFTER BEING HURT: SPECIAL GUEST PAUL YOUNG

The same way a loving father feels toward his children – that's but a sample of your tender feelings toward us, your beloved children, who live in awe of you. You know all about us, inside and out. You are mindful that we're made from dust.

-PSALM 103:13-14

SUMMARY

In this episode, Justin and Blair have a raw dialogue with Paul Young, author of *The Shack*, about his own shortcomings as a father and his road to restoration. Paul discusses the difference between forgiveness and reconciliation. He reveals the painful cost that he and his family paid because of his hiding and clinging to secrets.

Hearing the humble words of Young's process will challenge you to come out of hiding and find freedom from the secrets in your own world.

QUESTIONS FROM THE EPISODE

1. What secrets do I have that I believe would disqualify me from love?

2. Why do I believe these hidden places would disqualify me?

3. How would taking ownership and being completely honest with the people around me be a benefit?

4. Have I ever experienced my parents taking ownership for their mistakes and problems? What did that look like? If not, how did that hurt me?

_____
_____
_____
_____
_____
_____
_____
_____
_____
_____

5. Do I avoid taking ownership for my mistakes or the way I affect others? If so, why?

_____
_____
_____
_____
_____
_____
_____

6. Many opt out of forgiving because they think it condones the hurtful behavior and gives permission to do it again. Because of that, unforgiveness is used to create a boundary to protect from future pain. Where have I held on to unforgiveness for the sake of self-protection?

_____
_____
_____
_____
_____

7. Paul talked about surrendering his need to control and choosing to trust God. Is there a place in my life where I am afraid to be out of control? Why? How does this affect my life? What could my life look like and feel like if I lived with trust? How would my thought life change?

_____

_____

_____

_____

_____

_____

_____

_____

_____

8. What areas in my life need restoration? (Example: *Paul needed restoration in sexuality.*)

_____

_____

_____

_____

_____

_____

9. What relationships in my life need reconciliation? (Example: *Paul needed reconciliation with his wife and kids.*)

_____

_____

_____

_____

_____

_____

10. If I am making destructive decisions, how is that connected to my wounding? (Example: *Paul's destructive decisions in sexuality were connected to his unresolved childhood pain.*)

_____
_____
_____
_____
_____
_____
_____
_____
_____
_____
_____
_____
_____
_____
_____
_____

CONNECTING TO GOD AS FATHER

1. In what areas do you believe God is disappointed in you? (Example: *Porn addiction, yelling at my kids, not praying enough, not loving others enough, ect.*)

   _____
   _____
   _____
   _____

2. Would you allow God to meet you in the areas where you feel shame with Him? If not, what would keep you from taking that step?

   _____
   _____
   _____
   _____

3. If you're scared to invite Him in, or don't know how, here's an example of a simple prayer to say. "*God, I know that I am imperfect, but Your word says, 'Nothing can separate me from your love.' So, I invite You to love me in the areas that I think are unlovable or disappointing to you.*"

   Imagine the kindest person you know, and imagine God as kinder than him or her. With that picture in your mind, read these statements over yourself as if Father God is speaking them over you:

   - I am sorry you feel sad
   - I am sorry you feel alone
   - I see how hard you're trying
   - I am sorry you feel scared
   - I can tell you care so much
   - You are going to be okay
   - I love you where you are
   - I've seen your pain, and I am with you in the struggle
   - I will never leave you
   - I am proud of you

ACTIVATIONS

ACTIVATION ONE:

Make a list of choices, beliefs, or experiences in your life that you have kept hidden from most people because you believe that if they found out they would no longer love you.

Find safe friends or mentors to share these secrets and fears with.

ACTIVATION TWO:

Are there any places where you have hurt people and not apologized or taken responsibility? If specific instances come to mind, take note of them.

Start by having a conversation with God. Here's a simple prayer, *"Father God, please forgive me for . . ."* Tell Him you receive His forgiveness. Then take a moment to say out loud, *"I forgive myself for . . ."* Imagine yourself letting go of any shame that you've carried from this situation. Then picture yourself being fully embraced by Father God, where you feel fully accepted and loved by Him.

After you have asked for forgiveness from Father God and forgiven yourself, then go and apologize to the people you hurt along the way.

> "PAIN HAS A WAY OF CLIPPING OUR WINGS SO WE FORGET WE WERE EVER CREATED TO FLY."
>
> — PAUL YOUNG

NOTES

EPISODE SIX

CONFRONTING OUR FATHERS: HOPE FOR HEALING AND CONNECTION

Joseph had his chariot made ready and went to Goshen to meet his father Israel. As soon as Joseph appeared before him, he threw his arms around his father and wept for a long time.

-GENESIS 46:29 (NIV)

SUMMARY

In this episode, Justin and Blair are joined by fellow Life Consultant, Marcus Miller. Marcus vulnerably shares his journey of facing childhood sorrow that arose from his relationship with his dad.

Together, they give insights on how to start the process of dialoguing honestly with our fathers. They also reveal key practical tools to navigate healthy confrontation with our fathers in order to build trust, love, and connection.

QUESTIONS FROM THE EPISODE

1. When we experience suffering, we often try to avoid future pain by learning to control others. Where am I using control in my relationships with others in order to keep them from hurting or disappointing me?

2. Do I view people around me as generally powerful or powerless? Do I view others as emotionally healthy or unhealthy?

3. Am I okay with people being in emotional distress? Why or why not?

4. Where do I see myself trying to protect those around me? Do they need my protection, or would it be healthier for them to learn to protect themselves?

5. Have I grieved the pain from my relationship with my dad (and/or older men)? What areas do I have unresolved sorrow? If there are places of unprocessed hurt, what do I need to do to face the pain, grieve it, and release it?

6. Ideally, in what areas would I want God or healthy men to affirm me?

7. What are three practical steps I could take in the next week to pursue healing with my father or any father figures in my life?

8. Are there areas where I need to adjust the expectations I have of him in order to be more in line with the "reality" of where my father is relationally in his life? Are there any ways that I could healthily invite my dad further into my life?

_____
_____
_____
_____
_____
_____
_____

9. Are there places that my dad is trying his best to love me that I have not paid attention to or acknowledged?

_____
_____
_____
_____
_____

10. Do I tell my dad/father figure the things I am thankful for that he does well? If not, why?

_____
_____
_____
_____
_____

> **"SOMETIMES FEELINGS AREN'T RATIONAL, BUT THAT DOESN'T MEAN THEY'RE NOT VALID."**

CONNECTING TO GOD AS FATHER

1. Do you believe Father God wants to participate in your life? What activities in your life would you like to experience God's presence in? Would you be willing to invite Him to participate in every area of your life? If so, here is an example of a prayer. *"Papa, I invite You to reveal Yourself and to be present in every area of my life."*

_____
_____
_____
_____
_____
_____

2. Make a list of five moments where you felt God was participating in your story. (Example: *He gave me a business idea, gave me a dream that gave me clarity, brought a good friend into my life, helped me find something I really wanted on sale, etc.*)

1. _____
_____
_____

2. _____
_____
_____

3. _____
_____
_____

4. _____
_____
_____

5. _____
_____
_____

ACTIVATIONS

ACTIVATION ONE:

Find three places that your father or father figure has loved you well, and let him know. If you don't have someone that has loved you well, find a father figure in your life, and tell him three things he is doing that positively affect the world around him.

ACTIVATION TWO:

If it seems safe and you want to build further connection with your father, let him know that you would like to deepen your relationship. Ask him if he's interested in finding ways to get to know one another better. If he says yes, have ideas that you can suggest to do together.

Example: *Ask your dad to listen to an episode of The Liberation Project, read a book, or watch a TV show like This Is Us, and process them afterward. Set up a weekly get-together where you purposely invest in your bond. Take time to ask and answer some of these get-to-know-you questions, or feel free to write your own.*

GET-TO-KNOW-YOU QUESTIONS:
1. Given the choice of anyone in the world, who would you want as a dinner guest?
2. Would you like to be famous? If so, what would you like to be famous for?
3. Before making a telephone call, do you ever rehearse what you are going to say? Why?
4. What would constitute a "perfect" day for you?
5. What is your favorite memory of a birthday?
6. If you were able to live to the age of 90 and retain either the mind or body of a 30-year-old for the last 60 years of your life, which would you want?
7. Do you have a secret hunch about how you will die?
8. What is one of the biggest things you have overcome?
9. For what in your life do you feel most grateful?
10. If you could change anything about the way you were raised, what would it be?
11. What is one thing that you wish you could change about your past?
12. If you could wake up tomorrow having gained any one quality or ability, what would it be?

13. If a crystal ball could tell you the truth about yourself, your life, the future or anything else, what would you want to know?
14. Is there something that you've dreamed of doing for a long time? Why haven't you done it?
15. What is the greatest accomplishment of your life?
16. What do you value most in a friendship?
17. What is one of your most treasured memories?
18. What is one of the biggest heartaches that you have had to overcome?
19. If you knew that in one year you would die suddenly, would you change anything about the way you are now living? Why?
20. What does friendship mean to you?
21. What roles do love and affection play in your life?
22. What do you consider a positive characteristic of the other person? Share a total of five items.
23. How close and warm is your family? Do you feel your childhood was happier than other people's?
24. How do you feel about your relationship with your mother?
25. Make three true "we" statements each. For instance, "We are both in this room feeling..."
26. Complete this sentence: "I wish I had someone with whom I could share . . ."
27. If you were going to become a close friend with your parent/child, what would be important for him or her to know?
28. What do you like about your parent/child? Tell them and be very honest, saying things that you might not say to someone you've just met.
29. What was an embarrassing moment in your life? Share with your partner.
30. When did you last cry in front of another person? By yourself? Why did you cry?
31. What are five things that you are proud of your parent/child for?
32. If you were to die this evening with no opportunity to communicate with anyone, what would you most regret not having told someone? Why haven't you told them yet?
33. Your house, containing everything you own, catches fire. After saving your loved ones and pets, you have time to safely make a final dash to save any one item. What would it be? Why?
34. Share a personal problem and ask your parent/child advice on how he or she might handle it. Also, ask your partner to reflect back to you how you seem to be feeling about the problem you have chosen.

NOTES

EPISODE SEVEN

LAYING TO REST OUR FATHER WOUNDS

He will restore the hearts of the fathers to their children and the hearts of the children to their fathers.

-MALACHI 4:6 (NASB)

SUMMARY

In this tender and heart-wrenching episode, Justin bares his soul in the midst of processing the loss of his grandfather, Arnie. While celebrating his grandfather's life and acknowledging his shortcomings, Justin shares the beautiful story of reconciliation they experienced toward the end of Arnie's life.

This episode will give you the courage to be radically honest with your father. It will challenge you to forgive him for his failures and fill you with hope that true healing can infuse every wounded area.

QUESTIONS FROM THE EPISODE

1. As I heard Justin process his relationship with his grandfather, how was I affected? How does his story relate to my own life or relationships?

2. Do certain people in my life evoke anger or intense emotion when I think about them? Who are they? Why do I associate pain with them? Why do I believe they acted the way they did toward me?

3. Are there conversations I am afraid to have with others? Why are these conversations "off limits"? What do I believe will happen?

4. How were confrontations modeled to me as a child? How did it affect my approach and beliefs about confrontation?

5. Do I believe confrontation is healthy or unhealthy? Why do I believe that? Do I have unspoken rules about confronting parents, grandparents, and authority figures? If so, what are they?

6. Do I believe it's more loving to make someone happy than to be honest? If so, where did I learn that?

7. Do I think that confrontation is the end of relationship rather than an invitation for more connection? If so, why?

8. How could being more honest in my relationships improve them?

9. Where have I been honest and it worked out for the better?

10. How can being honest in my relationships help me step into being a powerful person? (Example: *I don't have to avoid people. I don't always feel traumatized with others.*)

CONNECTING TO GOD AS FATHER

Write a letter of what you think Father God might say to you, from the perspective of Him being a truly loving father figure. Be sure to include what He is proud of, characteristics He enjoys in you, and how He wants to relate to you.

DEDICATED TO ARNIE STUMVOLL
NOV 8, 1932 — MAY 14, 2016

"MY GRANDFATHER HAD THESE MOMENTS WHEN HE WANTED TO SHOW 'I LOVE YOU,' BUT HE DIDN'T KNOW HOW TO SAY IT."

ACTIVATIONS

ACTIVATION ONE:

Where have you been avoiding honesty in a current relationship due to a fear of conflict? Take time in the next week to share something that you have been afraid to share with this person.

ACTIVATION TWO:

Do you have a large place of pain from a relationship in your life, like Justin had with his grandpa? If so, create a time to vulnerably share with the person who caused you pain.

If that's not possible, find a safe person that you trust. Ask them to sit in front of you and to pretend that they are the person who hurt you. Now imagine them as that person who hurt you. Tell them how you felt and how you were affected by the interactions with them.

Example: *Let's say Justin's grandpa was unwilling to have that conversation. In that event, Justin would sit with Blair, and Blair would pretend to be Justin's grandpa. Justin would say, "Grandpa, you were a really harsh man. I felt really scared of you throughout my childhood. Your aggression made it feel really unsafe to be around you, etc."*

If the other person is up for it, they can lovingly respond in a validating way on behalf of the one you felt hurt by.

Example: *Blair looks at Justin and says, "Justin, I'm so sorry for being a harsh man. I'm sorry you felt scared and that I didn't feel safe to be around. Please forgive me for the pain I caused you."*

NOTES

EPISODE EIGHT

STORIES OF GOOD FATHERS

Do you know of any parent who would give his hungry child, who asked for food, a plate of rocks instead? Or when asked for a piece of fish, what parent would offer his child a snake instead? If you, imperfect as you are, know how to lovingly take care of your children and give them what's best, how much more ready is your heavenly Father to give wonderful gifts to those who ask him?

-MATTHEW 7:9-11

SUMMARY

A father's love has the power to shape our identity and heal our wounds. In this episode, Justin, Abi, and Blair share inspiring stories of good fathers that have the potential to shape you and heal you as well.

Whether these stories remind you of times in your life when you were greatly loved by a father or whether they reveal a place where you have never known a father's love, get ready to experience a new found hope in fathers.

QUESTIONS FROM THE EPISODE

1. What are three positive stories where a father figure has impacted me? What are the feelings I had during these moments? It is so important to meditate on moments of love - to think about and remember specific details and emotions as if it were happening again. (Shawn Achor has some great resources if you want more information on why it is so important to meditate on the good experiences we've had.)

   _____
   _____
   _____
   _____
   _____
   _____
   _____
   _____
   _____
   _____
   _____
   _____

2. In Josh's story with his son, Titus, he gave Titus permission to have emotions. Are there areas in my life where I need to give myself permission to have emotions in ways my father never did? If so, what are they?

   _____
   _____
   _____
   _____
   _____
   _____

3. Are there instances where I'm really hard on myself when I make mistakes because I didn't have a father who was kind when I made mistakes? How can I be kind, compassionate, and patient with myself regardless of how I grew up? (Example: *I'm really hard on myself when I forget things. I could be compassionate and patient the next time I forget something and tell myself that it isn't high stakes and that I'm worthy of love no matter what.*)

4. Recall a moment where an authority figure was kind to you when you made a mistake.

5. Where are the places I have taken my father's negative behaviors personally (either toward me or my family)? Can I see that his behavior is a reflection of how he treats himself and not a reflection of my worth? How so? (Example: *Blair's story of the dad who couldn't love his kids well because he didn't love himself well.*)

6. What are several movies or TV shows I have watched that display a father's affection that I needed as a kid? What moments impacted me? (Example: *Blair talking about the movie, We Bought a Zoo, and how it impacted him.*)

_____
_____
_____
_____
_____
_____
_____
_____
_____
_____
_____
_____
_____

7. When is a time that a father told me he was proud of me? What was he proud of? Do I tell myself what I'm proud of on a regular basis? What am I proud of when I think of myself?

_____
_____
_____
_____
_____
_____
_____
_____
_____
_____
_____

8. Have I seen fathers who love their kids well and are seeking ways to "engage" with their children's lives? What impacted me about the ways they love their children?

9. When Justin's dad helped him build the table, he was intentionally trying to be patient and follow through on his promise in ways he didn't in the past. Are there places in my life where I can see that my father has tried to mend past mistakes? If so, what are they?

10. What stood out as healing to my heart and mind during the validation and affirmation portion of this episode?

CONNECTING TO GOD AS FATHER

1. What do you believe Father God wants for your life?

_____
_____
_____
_____
_____

2. What are ways you were able to see God as father more clearly from hearing these stories of good fathers?

_____
_____
_____
_____
_____
_____
_____

ACTIVATIONS

ACTIVATION ONE:

Make a list of things that you believe a good father would do for a child he loves. Now take that list and change it into declarations of how you want to treat yourself.

Example: *A good father is gentle and kind when his child makes a mistake.*
Declaration: *Everyday, I am becoming more gentle and kind to myself when I make mistakes.*

Example: *A good father verbally affirms how proud he is of his child when he sees the child tries their best.*
Declaration: *I am so good at verbally affirming myself for doing my best regardless of the results.*

Read these declarations over yourself every day for 21 days.

ACTIVATION TWO:

Choose three declarations from the list you made in Activation #1 and purposefully put them into action this week.

Example: *A good father verbally affirms how proud he is of his child when he sees his child try their best.* This week purposefully notice and affirm yourself anytime you have done your best at something.

ACTIVATION THREE:

If you believe there is something in your life (choices you have made, thoughts you have, experiences that happened to you) that keeps you from feeling loved, have an open and vulnerable conversation with a parental figure that feels safe and loving. Share this thing with him, as well as your fear of not being loved for it.

> "ONE FATHER WAS NEVER MEANT TO DO ALL OF THE WORK OF FATHERING A CHILD; IT HAS TO BE A COMMUNITY EFFORT OF MEN."

NOTES

EPISODE NINE — BONUS EPISODE

RETURNING TO CHILDLIKENESS

My father and mother abandoned me. I'm like an orphan!
But you took me in and made me yours.
-PSALM 27:10

SUMMARY

Every once in a while things need to be changed up. Yay for fun surprises in the middle of this series! So, in this episode we get to listen to Abi speak at a live event. She shares her journey of learning to posture her heart as a child again. When you have grown up too fast or didn't feel like you could trust authorities, it can be easy to become independent and lose your childlikeness. In the journey of healing father wounds, it is vitally important that we learn to posture ourselves in vulnerability again.

And because this is a bonus, that means no homework for this episode! The Father is always working on our behalf. He can do as much when we are relaxing as He can when we are digging deep.

Listen, enjoy, and take a breather.

> "WHEREVER YOU HAD TO STEP OUT OF CHILDHOOD DUE TO PAIN OR DISCONNECTION, A PART OF YOU GETS STUCK AT THAT AGE."

EPISODE TEN

FATHER GOD

"I will be a true Father to you, and you will be my beloved sons and daughters," says the Lord Yahweh Almighty.

-2 CORINTHIANS 5:18

SUMMARY

How you view Father God directly affects not only how you treat yourself, but also how you show up to the world around you. God is often perceived as being angry, disapproving, impatient, and disappointed. This can result in torment and struggle for many people.

In this session, Justin and Abi, along with special guest, Forest Kerbow, share personal stories that reveal Father God as loving, joyful, kind, patient, comforting, and trustworthy. Get ready to see how God wants to father us in all seasons of our lives.

QUESTIONS FROM THE EPISODE

1. How have I viewed the Father's thoughts and attitudes toward others and me? (Example: *He is a passive observer, He is disappointed, He loves it when people work really hard for him, He is kind.*) Where do I think those views of Him stemmed? (Example: *Authority figures, parents, pastors, TV/media, culture, etc.*)

2. Are there areas in my life where I've tried to earn God's love and approval? If so, what did that look like?

3. Is there a balance in my life where I am experiencing God directly and through other people? If either of these places are lacking, invite God to bring balance into the way you experience Him.

4. What are three ways I have experienced God through people? What are three ways I have experienced God directly?

5. Sometimes when we look back, we can see that God was with us even when we couldn't necessarily sense Him. What are some seasons in my life where God was fathering me even though I was unaware of Him in the moment? How did He father me?

6. Were there times in my life where I believed the lie that because I didn't get what I wanted, God didn't love me? What were those experiences? (Example: *I have been waiting for a long time for a spouse, I didn't get a job I really wanted, etc.*)

- Our misperceptions of God can lead to anger and pain. Looking back, how was I possibly seeing Him inaccurately? (Example: *He grieved with me when I had health issues. He is present with me in my journey of desiring a wife and has empathy for me when I feel alone.*)

- Would you be willing to invite God into your disappointment to show you His compassion or perspective? If so, here is an example of a prayer. *"God, I invite You into any area where I have held disappointment, anger, or sadness toward You. I welcome Your love and goodness to soften my heart where my hurt has created separation or distance between us."*

7. Are there times in my life when I felt disciplined by God but I interpreted it through shame? (Example: *When I looked at porn, I felt like He was saying I was an idiot and a failure or that He couldn't love me or bless me.*)

- What did He correct me on? (Example: *Porn usage*)
- How did I interpret his correction? (Example: *I'm a failure and an idiot.*)
- If you weren't interpreting His discipline through your shame, how was His correction an invitation to deeper intimacy and an abundant life? (Example: *He was inviting me into real intimacy with Him and others, instead of a fake substitute in porn.*)

ACTIVATIONS

ACTIVATION ONE:

Because of our sense of abandonment and fear, many of us have a tendency to believe the Father is not an invested Dad. We assume that He is not going to provide for us, not only in our needs, but in our desires as well. This perspective often stems from focusing on what we don't have, which blinds us to what we *do have*. Dissatisfaction then leads us to think that God doesn't care.

One of the best ways to get in touch with His provision in your life is to practice being really thankful for what He has already provided. For this activation, take some time and make a list of *all* of the ways that God has provided for you throughout your life. List everything from the seemingly small things all the way to major life events. Notice the emotions and thoughts that come up as you do this exercise. What does this list evoke?

ACTIVATION TWO:

For the next week, spend at least 5-10 minutes daily envisioning God as loving, delighted, and joyful in interacting with you.

If you are having difficulty seeing Him this way and having it feel real, ask God questions. *"Who am I seeing instead of You? Where is this root belief about You specifically coming from?"*

After you feel like He has shown you what is getting in the way, invite Father to show you how He truly is. Give Him permission to remove the inaccurate views of Him. Ask, *"God, how have You been trying to connect with me in ways that I've been unaware of?"*

> **"GOD IS SO REDEMPTIVE THAT HE WILL USE ANY SCENARIO AS AN OPPORTUNITY TO SHOW UP AND LOVINGLY FATHER US."**

NOTES

EPISODE ELEVEN

COMPASSION FOR FATHERS: GUEST DANNY MARTINEZ

Praise be to the God and Father of our Lord Jesus Christ, the Father of compassion and the God of all comfort, who comforts us in all our troubles, so that we can comfort those in any trouble with the comfort we ourselves receive from God.

-2 CORINTHIANS 1:3-4 (NIV)

SUMMARY

In this episode, special guest Danny Martinez shares openly and vulnerably about his journey of being a father. He recounts his personal pains and struggles, his failures, his wins, and how the pain from his relationship with his own father impacted it all.

Throughout this conversation, Danny imparts the wisdom gained in his fatherhood process as he's learned how to let go of unrealistic expectations, choose self-compassion, and live with hope for restoration.

QUESTIONS FROM THE EPISODE
IF YOU HAVE CHILDREN

*For mothers going through this series, these questions can apply to you as well by exchanging the "fathering" terms below with "mothering/parenting" terms.

1. What are five strengths and two weaknesses I feel I have as a father?

2. Are there any ways that I am trying to fill my own needs in fathering my children? If so, how has that affected my children's lives and their interactions and experiences with me?

3. What are the ways in my fatherhood journey that I'm similar to my own dad? How might some of the wounds from my own father affect the way I behave as a parent?

4. What are some ways I've tried to make up for the lack I experienced with my own father as I parent my children (either positive or negative)?

5. What kind of expectations do I have/feel:
- From society about what I'm supposed to be as a father?
- Of myself as a father?
- From my spouse or the mother of my children?
- From my children?
- Which of the above expectations do I have shame about that can lead to the conclusion that I'm not enough?

6. What feelings and thoughts come up as I process how I have hurt or could hurt my children, even when I've tried my best and my intentions were and are good?

- How have I chosen to respond to these feelings when they've come up before? (Example: *I deflect my shame and I blame the people around me, I shut down and compartmentalize so I don't have to feel it, etc.*)
- How can I better handle these thoughts to benefit my children and me in the future?
- Can I accept that no matter how good my intentions are, I will cause pain in my family's life? If the answer is no, what do I need to do to get to a place where I can accept this?

7. How do I believe my children have experienced me? Am I willing to have a conversation(s) with them to ask them this question?

- Have they had blame and resentment toward me? If so, in what areas?
- What will help me respond with compassion and understanding to their feedback? (Example: *Forgive myself, listen without reacting, make it about their feelings not my shame, etc.*)
- Am I expecting feedback that is going to make me feel okay? (If yes, you may want to reassess why you're asking them.)

8. Ask God, "*What are the areas where You are proud of me as a father?*"

9. How do I see God as a father to me? How have these views affected me in fathering my own children?

10. What are some ways that other men have fathered me throughout my life?

ACTIVATIONS

ACTIVATION ONE (FOR PARENTS):

It can be easy at times to see all of the ways you may have fallen short as a father. Yes, it's important to [compassionately] be aware of your weaknesses so that you have the opportunity to step into more growth. It is equally important, however, to be aware of your "Dad Wins".

Write down ten dad wins. (Moments or decisions that you feel really proud of.)

Then take 5-10 minutes once a week to reflect and add to your list. (Ask God if He has anything He wants to add to the list that you may have initially forgotten.)

_____
_____
_____
_____
_____
_____
_____
_____
_____
_____
_____
_____
_____
_____
_____
_____
_____
_____
_____
_____
_____
_____

ACTIVATION TWO (FOR PARENTS):

As each father becomes more in touch with his authentic self, it becomes easier to discover the unique qualities he possesses in fathering his children.

Write down ten personal strengths that you have as a father. Post your list of strengths somewhere you will see it often (bathroom mirror, car, etc.) to help remind yourself that you are a good dad, that God is so proud of you, and that your family gets to benefit because of who you are.

QUESTIONS FROM THE EPISODE
IF YOU DO NOT HAVE CHILDREN

1. How did hearing Danny share from a father's perspective affect me? How did it impact the view I have of fathering? Did it affect how I see my dad's mistakes?

2. How is God different than my father?

3. What are some ways that other men have fathered me throughout my life?

4. Are there areas in life I need to adjust the expectations of my father in order to be more in line with the "reality" of where my father is emotionally and relationally? If so, which ones?

5. How might some of the wounds from my father affect the way I behave as a parent if I choose to have children one day? What steps do I need to take to resolve them?

6. Do I have compassion on my father? If not, why?

7. How did my dad's childhood affect how he has fathered me?

8. Where do I see that my dad has tried wholeheartedly to do his best?

9. What are my dad's strengths as a father?

CONNECTING TO GOD AS FATHER

1. When you picture Father God, do you picture Him smiling, distant, or frowning?

2. What are the areas in your life you believe would make God smile? (Example: *When I am kind, when I am awkward, my corny jokes, when I'm thankful, etc.*)

3. What are the areas of your life that would make God laugh? (Example: *When I make up silly songs, when I laugh at my own jokes, when I mix up the Bible character's names because of my dyslexia, when I fall asleep while I'm praying, etc.*)

ACTIVATIONS

ACTIVATION (FOR EVERYONE):

Throughout this series we have focused on looking honestly at the pain from our fathers and finding ways to grieve and heal. In this activation, as we reflect on our fathers, we will write a unique letter to them through the eyes of compassion.

Pain is something that gets passed down from generation to generation. The areas where our fathers hurt us are often because they were wounded as well.

Example: *If no one affirmed him, he may not know how to affirm you. If no one taught him to be present, he may not know how to be present with you.*

In this activation we want you to write a letter from God to your father. We want you to imagine all of the things that your father needed to hear from his father that he might have never heard.

Example: *"Son, I believe in you. I'm so sorry that your dad abandoned you. You are worth sticking around for. You are worth my time and energy. You are interesting and fun to be around. You are worth fighting for and worth believing in. It's ok for you to be sad sometimes. You have permission to feel emotions. You are not being weak by having emotions. I'm so sorry that you never heard me say that I love you. You are so easy to love . . ."*

After writing this letter, read it out loud to yourself as a declaration over your dad. Talk to God and ask Him to help you see your dad through His lens of compassion. Pray and ask God to bring healing and love to your dad's heart.

_____
_____
_____
_____
_____
_____
_____
_____
_____

NOTES

EPISODE TWELVE

MOVING FORWARD: STEPS TO FORGIVENESS

Has God graciously forgiven you? Then graciously forgive one another in the depths of Christ's love.

-EPHESIANS 4:32

SUMMARY

In this episode, Justin and Abi dissect key aspects of what it looks like to enter into forgiveness and recognize that it is a process with no clear-cut, linear path. This frees us up to go on a unique, personal journey with Father God to discover how to get out of hurts and offenses that have caused us pain.

Included in this episode are multiple approaches in the forgiveness journey, meant to empower you to let go of anger, bitterness, and resentment in order to move toward increasing compassion and healing.

12 QUESTIONS FROM THE EPISODE

1. What are some crucial "debts" with my dad that I have become aware of in this series? What are the ripple effects of those debts? (Example: *Being abused by a male authority figure. Not only are you dealing with the pain of the event itself, but also the shame, the struggle with low self-esteem, hatred towards men, and various other issues.*)

2. Have I validated that the debt owed to me matters? (Example: *It matters that my dad abandoned me and that I have had to fight for myself for so many years.*)

3. Do I believe that my father can somehow repay me for the pain I've experienced?

    - If so, what are the ways I have believed or expected him to repay me?
    - How has this contributed to me feeling powerless with him?
    - How has this affected my ability to forgive him?
    - It's time to admit that he can't pay you back for what he owes you. Write out, *"Dad, I realize that you cannot repay the debt you owe me, and I will quit asking you to pay it."*
    - Invite God to pay the debt your dad owes you, and imagine yourself writing "canceled" over the debt.

4. Do I truly believe that what Jesus did at the Cross was enough to cover the debts of others and myself? Have I fully allowed myself to see that God has completely covered every mistake I've made? Do I see the need for my own forgiveness from Him?

5. Ask God: "*Are there any areas where I haven't forgiven myself? Where have I not received forgiveness from You?*"

- Write down a list of the debts you think you owe.

- Read **Matthew 18:23-27**:
  "*There once was a king who had servants who had borrowed money from the royal treasury. He decided to settle accounts with each of them. As he began the process, it came to his attention that one of his servants owed him one billion dollars. So he summoned the servant before him and said to him, 'Pay me what you owe me.' When his servant was unable to repay his debt, the king ordered that he be sold as a slave along with his wife and children and every possession they owned as payment toward his debt. The servant threw himself face down at his master's feet and begged for mercy. 'Please be patient with me. Just give me more time and I will repay you all that I owe.'* **Upon hearing his pleas, the king had compassion on his servant, and released him, and forgave his entire debt.**"

- Write canceled over each debt.

- Visualize God having deep compassion for you and being excited to pay the debt you owe so that you can be free.

- If you have asked for forgiveness for a specific debt, speak forgiveness over yourself. (It's important to speak truth out loud because our brain responds powerfully to the words it hears our own voice say. Our words have the power to train our brain.) The following is an example, not a rule or magic phrase of how to connect with and receive forgiveness for yourself: "*God, thank You for paying the debt for me. I receive Your compassion and forgiveness for (insert specific debt). Thank you for fully canceling my debt. I give myself permission to receive your compassion, forgive myself and never carry the burden of this again.*"

- Write a prayer of blessing over yourself.

_____
_____
_____
_____
_____
_____
_____
_____

6. What does it cost me to hold onto unforgiveness toward my father? Is this serving me?

7. Have I been afraid that my father will get access to me if I forgive him? Do I believe that I have to let down all of my boundaries and be close to him if I forgive him? If so, what are some healthy boundaries that I can put in place?

8. Since the offense took place, are there ways that I've continued to play the "victim" role? What are those ways?

9. Are there ways that I've been playing the "judge" through not forgiving my dad?

- Ask: *"God, how do You feel about the 'little kid' that is hurting inside of my dad?"*
- How am I similar to this person (in my humanity)? How have I also operated in anger, fear, control, betrayal, self-protection, blame, etc., toward others?

_____

_____

_____

_____

_____

_____

_____

_____

_____

10. What does it look like for me to take ownership for the part that I've played in agreeing with and perpetuating the beliefs (lies) that came with the offense? (Example: *Abi's story of being cut out of someone's life… what that person did was hurtful, but it was Abi's pre-existing shame that amplified the pain of the situation.*) (Example: *My father always said that I was stupid. Once I was grown I continued to talk to myself with his words. Now I need to take ownership for how I hurt myself with the words I originally heard from him.*)

_____

_____

_____

_____

_____

_____

_____

_____

_____

11. Write a prayer to bless your father.

_____
_____
_____
_____
_____
_____
_____
_____
_____

A FORGIVENESS ROADMAP:

- Thoroughly take account of the "debt" (offense, pain, etc.) that is "owed" to you, as well as the effects of the debt.
- Recognize and come to terms with the reality that the other person cannot repay the debt (no matter how much they may reconcile). They cannot change what has already been done.
- Acknowledge that Jesus' action at the cross was enough to cover the debt. Ask Him to pay it back and heal the pain in your heart through His Love.
- Ask yourself if you've fully allowed yourself to receive God's forgiveness for all the mistakes you've made. Receive His forgiveness in any areas that He shows you.
- Ask God to show you how to see the "little kid" inside the person that hurt you . . . the kid that is carrying so much pain.
- Take ownership for any ways where you've acted like the "judge" and for the part that you've played in agreeing with and perpetuating the beliefs (lies) that came with the offense/offender.
- Pray for them to be blessed.

CONNECTING TO GOD AS FATHER

1. Ask God: *"God, what did You feel for me when the offense(s) took place?"*

   _____
   _____
   _____
   _____

2. Ask God: *"What are some of the things You love about me?"*

   _____
   _____
   _____
   _____

3. Ask God: *"Do You have good things for me? What are they?"*

   _____
   _____
   _____
   _____

4. Ask God: *"What are the reasons you believe in me?"*

   _____
   _____
   _____
   _____

5. What do you believe your relationship with God would be like if you believed you were fully forgiven and loved by Father God?

_____
_____
_____
_____
_____
_____
_____
_____
_____
_____
_____
_____
_____

Take a minute to imagine God, with a smile on His face, delighting in forgiving you.

ACTIVATIONS

ACTIVATION ONE:

Tell some close friends about the journey of forgiveness you went on through the previous questions. Share with them the places you forgave yourself and where you forgave others. If you are struggling with forgiving, have them pray for you. Then pray with them to bless the person that you are forgiving.

ACTIVATION TWO:

Is there anyone that you need to go to and ask for forgiveness? If so, who? Go and do that.

> "FORGIVENESS HEALS AND RESTORES US. IT RELIEVES US FROM THE BURDEN WE ARE CARRYING."

NOTES

CONCLUSION

There you have it. Great job on completing this E-course!

As we said in the introduction, our heart for this series is to initiate a dialogue that engages healing. We hope that it helped you connect a few dots, feel some feelings, think some thoughts, forgive some wounds, and release some burdens.

All three of us have had seasons of looking at father wounds. The process we went through didn't mean that all of our daddy issues were resolved. The healing journey will continue to unfold throughout our lives. The grace for visiting these areas of our hearts will vary in each season and be unique for each individual.

For some, this may have just scratched the surface. Maybe there was only grace to face one facet of your relationship with your dad. That's okay! There is no pressure to do it all at once. Some of you may have found yourselves gutted and you may walk away with fingers crossed and hopes high that you'll never have to do that again. That's all right as well.

If there is more, there will be the grace to face it. The point is simply to keep your heart open to whatever God wants to visit or revisit. It's never "the same old thing". There will always be a fresh perspective when He issues the invitation.

As you've completed this series you may find yourself wanting more resources to continue your journey. If that's you, we recommend the following list of books and messages:

- "Redefined by Love"– Abi Stumvoll (Audio Series)
- "Unconditional"– Abi Stumvoll (Audio Series)
- "Wildly Free" – Abi Stumvoll (Audio Series)
- *The Shack* - Paul Young
- *Love Does* - Bob Goff
- *Everybody Always*– Bob Goff
- *Scary Close* - Donald Miller
- *Experiencing the Father's Embrace* - Jack Frost
- *A Return to Love* - Marianne Williamson
- *Baptism of Love* - Leif Hetland
- *Healing the Orphan Spirit* - Leif Hetland
- "The Inheritance"- Graham Cooke (YouTube Video)
- *Win+Win Parenting*– Seth Dahl
- *Keep Your Love On*– Danny Silk
- *Loving Your Kids On Purpose*– Danny Silk

As a follow up to this series, we also highly recommend *The Family Reconciliation Series* by *The Liberation Project* Podcast. It can be found on iTunes, Stitcher, and YouTube.

ONE-ON-ONE RESOURCES

There are a few coaches who are not only brilliant at helping people navigate through pain into wholeness but who have spent hours diving into healing pain in their own childhoods. These coaches have personal life experience as well as compassion and a natural intuition. We highly recommend them for any areas in your life where you want to experience more growth. For information regarding these coaches contact us at lfa@stumvollconsulting.com

If you have children, you may have realized that there are areas that need work in your own parenting. Most parents are completely overwhelmed and doing the best they know how. Reaching out to get help is one of the best things you can do for your children's futures. For information on parenting resources and coaches contact us at lfa@stumvollconsulting.com

Lastly, if you have testimonies you would like to share, or if you would like more information about one-on-one consulting with us, we can be contacted via email on our websites:

- www.justinstumvoll.com
- www.abistumvoll.com

Thanks for going on the journey with us. We hope you enjoyed it as much as we enjoyed making it.

Justin and Abi are internationally sought-after speakers and life consultants. They have spent over a decade facilitating emotional healing in the lives of individuals and groups and training others to do the same. In their podcast, *The Connected Life*, they share all of the raw and real details about how to have healthy connection with others, God, and yourself.

Their highest dream is to redefine love in practical and empowering ways. Their hope is that this love would restore and redeem marriages, families, and all the brokenhearted. Justin is also the author of *The Tree of Life*, an allegory of learning how to come alive wherever you are planted.